AUTUMN MAKES ME SING

Poems from the VOLE Books
Summer Poetry Competition 2024
selected by Kathryn Southworth

Edited by Janice Dempsey

Summer makes me drowsy.
Autumn makes me sing.

Dorothy Parker

AUTUMN MAKES ME SING
© Janice Dempsey (editor)
2024

Published by Dempsey & Windle under their VOLE imprint
15 Rosetrees
Guildford
Surrey
GU1 2HS
UK
01483 571164
dempseyandwindle.com

A catalogue record for this book is available from the British
Library
British Library Cataloguing-in-Publication Data
ISBN: 978-1-917101-08-0

Printed and bound in the UK

With gratitude to Kathryn Southworth,
who gave so generously of her time when judging
the VOLE Summer Competition 2024.

Contents

Judge's report

Reading through some 350 poems in a concentrated fashion is a humbling experience. Whilst poetry is not history or autobiography, it bears witness to both and poems are freighted with powerful memories, indignation at human behaviour, pity for the frailty of the human condition. – and even a fragile hopefulness. It is brave of us to write about these things and even braver to submit them to the vagaries of someone else's judgement. So, thanks are due to all who submitted to this competition and to Janice and Donall for this trust, and for giving me the privilege of exercising both an impartial critical eye and, necessarily, a personal predilection.

Amid poems about the seasons, art, ancestors, climate change and the natural world in all its amazing complexity, were elegy, observation and celebration, together with a rich feast of sensuous language about fabrics, food and vegetation. In the winning and commended poems there was more: a telling perspective, a unique angle of observation which moved both subject and execution from the ordinary to the memorable, intense or even remarkable. Where poems were less successful and did not reach the standards of this anthology, they did not have this kind of particularity on which to hang their feelings or ideas, or perhaps the language was less convincing as an authentic human voice. This was especially evident in the way some poems closed, where the attempt to round off (especially in a rhyme) could be too obvious or, in some cases, baffling.

Where last lines are effective, they give resonance to the whole poem, returning us to the title, understanding it again, as if for the first time. This is particularly true of the overall winning poem and the powerful metaphor in its title which raises a commonplace expression to the level of a telling symbol of hope. There are politics in this poem, and some attributions of prejudice which may be controversial and potentially deniable. However, not only does it focus on one of the most horrifying situations of our time, but its wider message is the indomitable human spirit embodied in a young boy making something literally radiant out of what is broken.

The second and third winners are both, in their different ways, about touch. Both have arresting openings and arrive at a fascinating full-circle in their conclusions, though something remarkable has happened in between and life will never be quite the same again. The commended poems have a sureness of touch, in the rendering of a sensuous moment, in the evocation of place and elegiac loss, or in the liberation of life after death.

In their different ways, be it wit, lyricism or emotional intensity, the poems which made it to this anthology are searching and challenging and, through their observation, they bear witness. Poems do not necessarily set out to do this, or display the scars of strain and effort but, if they work, this is what they do.

Kathryn Southworth
September 2024

JANET HATHERLEY

The light in his eyes

Here we are living in darkness and tragedy
the rockets falling on us. I looked at my twin nephews
saw only fear in their eyes. I thought of creating light.

Hussam Al-Attar, aged fifteen.

When the sun went down
Hussam and his family

sat in the dark
in the small glow of a gas lamp.

*

Next day at the scrap market
he found two fans, some wires.

Reuters said
he looks and sounds young for his age

as if all fifteen-year olds don't
look and sound young.

*

After the bombing of Al-Azha university
an Israeli soldier filmed himself on Tik Tok

mocking students. He said
For those asking why

there is no education in Gaza,
we bombed them. Oh, too bad.

That way you'll not be
engineers anymore.

*

The wind blows, the fans turn,
generate friction inside the dynamo.

A current travels
through the wires, lights up the tent.

*

Hussam wants to be an engineer
when he's older—

loves creating something
out of broken things.

9

SUE NORTON

Convent of San Marco, Florence

Each year the monks moved cells for a different biblical mural to contemplate,
all of them masterworks by Fra Angelico.

The monk I envy the most is the one
with the resurrection inside his door.

The painted scene almost smells of new beginnings;
red and white petals stipple the grass,
a green palm sprouts a feathered plume.

Mary Magdalene's on her knees at the black gape
of the tomb, freshly cut from white rock.
She's just found it's empty.

Christ has a hoe on his shoulder like the gardener she mistakes him for
and it's the moment he calls *Mary!*

and she drops to her knees, face bewildered, arms uplifted.
His hand, touched with red to show where
Friday's nail was hammered in, gestures away, face kind but

no - don't touch me. Christ side-steps
to avoid her clutch, but it's not a rejection, no
he's about to appoint her

Apostle to the Apostles, a messenger the men won't touch
for centuries, not believing

the newly risen Christ would show himself first
to an unreliable witness, to a woman.
The painted garden draws its astonished breath.

Third Prize

DEREK SELLEN

The Merchant in Autumn

For you, I recommend ..., said the merchant,
running his finger along the bolts of cloth,
pausing to study me, then back to the colours.
He swathed me in daffodil-yellow, wrapping
half my body, a shoulder to hip diagonal.
He appraised, rejected, tried lilacs and reds,
the most verdant greens. I moved to the mirror
but each time he whipped away the fabric
with sighs as if I disappointed. *Too rich*, he said,
too cold, too hot.
          In the deep recesses of his shop,
I saw steel-greys, thundercloud-blacks, arctic
gradations of white. I shivered to think
of the blizzard of silks on my skin. *Ah!*
now look at the bruised magnificence of these –
such phrases, such salesmanship, such commands –
they will warm you like sunshine late in the year,
bringing you peace. Acceptance. Madam, I say,
               they are our only choice,
these mulberries, these russets, these tarnished golds.

The clock on his wall chimed. I made excuses
and hurried out. In the market, the lying traders
called, offering cheap jewels, tinctures, dresses.
               Too rich,
he said in my ear, *too cold, too hot. Too soon, too late.*

PAUL McDONALD

Somewhere a Song is Frantic

after Malick Sidibé, 'Nuit de Noël (Happy Club),' 1963

These dancers cool the humid night
with style. The shyest eyes can see
beyond this slice of time, bewitched by
clever feet, hers bare as lovers' tongues.

These dancers would be sweethearts,
swans entwined for life if time
ticked on. A single beat would seal it:
hip-to-hip till movement matches meaning.

But look, a sudden slice of silence:
his necktie in mid-swing, her cotton dress
a frozen swish as stars forgo their slide
across the sky. Somewhere a song is frantic

to continue: a loudspeaker tethered to a
palm tree, a turntable mute on a
tabletop, paused with the Earth's spin.
We wait for time and heartbeats to begin.

Highly Commended

GILL LEARNER

Unmoored

I've not quite got the hang of this. Feet dangle –
a threat to sunflower heads. So I kick as I would
if in too deep. It works: I rise to skim the hedge,
and next door's holly scrapes my toes. I drift like
dandelion silk. I can look into other gardens, see
who grows veg, who prizes dahlias, who's mad
about sweet peas. And, tsk: that number 21's
got plastic grass. I twist towards the houses, peer
into windows, see Mick at 25 tapping on his keyboard.
I smile an ad wave as he looks up. But his gaze is focussed
far away. I paddle with my hands, glide along the street.

A gust whisks me west and south: high over suburbs
and across the Downs; I tread air by Uffington's White Horse
admiring its simplicity. Beyond Stonehenge, curves
the Jurassic Coast so, at last, the sea. Above the Exe
the breeze almost lets me drop, then buoys me up again,
westward, till I sink sweetly next to Lanyon Quoit – unsteady
I grab the capstone slab. From here I can see water
north and south, can fill my lungs with salty air. Suddenly
I hear Emma's voice, hushed but urgent: *Mum, Mum.*
Now Bruce's: *No! You know her wishes – DNR.*
Ems, we have to let her go.

Highly Commended

TRISHA TORRINGTON

You Missed Paris

After 'You Hated Spain' by Ted Hughes

You missed Paris.
It was one of the places you wanted to see,
to take your wife; to say you'd seen
the romantic heart of the Art Nouveau.

You missed tasting moules, baguettes, camembert,
and garlicky escargots, crepes and bavettes.
Would you have eaten them? You'd have stuck
to what you know, frites and maybe
a merguez or two, jambon, oeufs.
You missed the wine (you always thought it sour
but couldn't really taste it anyway,
only heavy tangs of salt and sugar).

You missed Paris.
Boulevards you couldn't stroll,
the Tuileries she'd have loved but
you wouldn't. The art galleries
you'd have merely glanced at.
Just to say it was something you'd done...
visited Paris with my mother,
a romantic weekend manqué.

But you had the idea of it.
After you were gone
we took her there for you.
A bus trip round the sights,
a *bateau mouche*, a trip
out to Versailles, on the *Petit Train*.
All she wanted was a prawn cocktail, a decent cup of tea.
She missed Paris, too.
Because she missed being there with you.

ROD WHITWORTH

August legs

After Richard Barnett

August has the loveliest legs
not like Marlene Dietrich
or even Cyd Charisse

August has the legs of Beryl Burton
August wants to turn pedals
And the legs of Tenzing Norkay
August wants to walk up hills

August wants to keep on doing it

TRICIA TORRINGTON

Madonna with Two Angels

Filippo Lippi sketches me in,
one of his many Madonnas.
He says I am like the white snow trees.
He says this is about family.
He wants us to be natural,
wear the halo as light.

Filippo says I am like golden blossom.
Pale fire he calls me,
says I am fine silk, precious material.
He wants stillness.
He says fold your hands like a butterfly
waiting in the light.

I say nuns know how to pray,
to put our palms together, to supplicate.
My fingers fall naturally to their old attitude
until my hands are so full of prayer
I cannot hold the child.
This painting is about family, and it is ours.

He traces his own face on the holy child,
paints Fillipino as one messenger of God.
Neither of them is an angel.
Obsessed with the virginal he wants
to show purity. I am no longer pure
for he has taken me; I bore his child.

In place of sanctity I offer contemplation,
In place of innocence - modesty, and he says
beauty wearing blue, Madonna's colour,
indigo as the mysterious night sky.
Filippo Lippi paints me in.
Madonna with two angels.

ROSIE BARRETT

Autumn is the Time for Babies

Just in time to be interesting at Christmas
Autumn babies have a whole winter
of rolling   crawling   cooed over by endless
loomings of great aunts and stubbles of uncles.

They take the sting out of all those cold
dank days of winter
after all the Christmas parties when
it seems the sun will never fully
rise again.

Springtime and the half yearlings gurgle
talk the language of babies the world over
intonation comes later.

Their summer's spent eating mud or if lucky
sand   being dunked in the waves
on a holiday by the sea.

Then Autumn again   maybe an Indian summer
when Gaia seems to give the world a second chance
and those babies stagger from table leg to chair

finally walking.

Autumn   when the prospect of another winter of war
makes leaders think hard   negotiate
and soldiers make the most of their home leave
and more babies.

ANDREW GEORGE

Sports Day

1. *The Nursery Race*

The starter's pistol fires and no-one moves.
Someone howls. Mimed at by the teachers,
children start to shuffle down the track.
One trips and falls and seven stop to help.
Half-way down three blonde-haired toddlers link
their arms, revolve and run back to the start.
In Lane 1, two boys in baggy kits
sit down and play a noisy game with fists.
The commentator's lapsed into silence.
The crowd mutate their cheers to conversation.
It's a great surprise when someone wins.
She's delighted with her gold rosette
and wants another for her friend, who's still
meandering towards the finish line.

2. *The Fathers' Race*

The trick is not to look as though you're trying.
Wear a suit as if you've just arrived,
you're running 'on a whim' to 'be a sport'.
At the gun, we charge across the field,
sharpened elbows pistoning away.
Half-way down the pacesetters drop back.
A young dad draws ahead and breasts the line.
He celebrates as if the world is watching,
then saunters off towards the coffee tent.
On the track, the injuries are awful.
Several have collapsed and I throw up.
One man sits and waves away assistance.
He'll need to work out later how to get
his ruptured tendon and his children home.

Retired Hurt

This, of course, is life-changing as well -
no white train to glide across the dance-floor,
the wedding guests astounding in their warmth,
no sudden piercing scream, no frail new body,
cut and weighed and thrust into his arms,
no organising cars and cool refreshments,
hoping that his eulogy is tender -
just a subtle swaying from the wine,
half a tear when thinking of the speeches
(that folk even remembered all those things!),
encumbered by an outsize card, a magnum,
a cricket bat that's signed by all the gang,
finding, as he struggles through the station,
the annual pass that will not be renewed.

PENNY BLACKBURN

Do Not Be Alarmed

The lampposts have started gathering on a night.
Not the new ones, they stay where they're put.
The ones that went unnoticed, unreplaced. Concrete

nudges to the memory. Mini-Brutalist monuments
dispersing sodium-hazy light. Always in old places –
down by the lock-ups, the back alley by the shops,

at the edge of the last field. The one half way
along the track, like a tiny pool of orange
would make that short-cut any safer. By this one

is where they all huddle, swan-necks bent together.
The light still doesn't stretch any further. The weight
of unopened black presses round them.

They don't care. They talk of whether art
is always political, what should be done
about colony collapse, the final frailties of God.

Clearly something is starting to happen
but the lampposts aren't saying what.

SHARRON GREEN

10 Things a Crime Scene Cleaner Should Know

1) You cannot remove ALL the blood

2) and blood is only a fraction of the issue

3) there's also tissue and bone.

4) Clients expect perfection

5) but the odour will linger,

6) and the room will remember.

7) Sometimes a spirit hovers,

8) staining the carpet with clues,

9) seeping into the floorboards.

10) You will never forget your first.

TINA COLE

Let's meet somewhere outside time and space

between the phoenix and her ashes on an evening when
the sky paints the sea in citrus and lime and tides rule

the moon, let's meet in a garden tumultuous and pungent
with colour where we engage with the voices of poplar

trees to make beautiful silence together. Let's float inside
a bottle of vintage Veuve Clicquot, in that moment of smile,

not smile on the dark side of a distant world, inside walls
that smell of something hidden beneath red flock

wallpaper, slip inside a mole skin coat, pockets filled
with Sobranie cocktail, arms made of smoke, get whipped

up at the marriage of strawberries and cream while headlights
reflect garnets and pirate treasure in puddles on psychedelic

tarmac. Let's meet when the Caucus race has just begun
and Alice only has Prozac in her pocket, take a trip

as the year prepares to wane, as the planet implodes,
let's light a candle, whisper a fierce prayer for each flame,

for each other, let them linger on the eyelashes of china dolls,
beneath the feathers of flightless birds, inside great aunt Maud's

satin corset whose silken cords are unravelling, allowing
her to breathe, allowing us to finally speak a similar language.

Bottle Tags and Fantasy

It's all in the way you look at things or so they say.
I remember them being purchased in some dusty
shop, how they glinted in the forty-watt light,
in amongst tarnished soup tureens and discarded
cutlery. The shop keeper with a fag stuck
to his yellowed lips and ashy cardigan. My hand
went out to instinctively trace the inscriptions,
whisky, gin, vermouth. Oh, that word, vermouth!
It was evenings in cerise silk pyjamas, something louche,
bohemian, a life away from corseted cares. Listening
to Chopin, Rachmaninov, nights at the Royal Opera House,
not the sixpenny stalls at the local Odeon. No, the life
I deserved sitting in a green Lloyd loom chair, wafting
about a Hampstead flat, thin and mysterious, smoking
something sweetly scented. I would have written
a clutch of acclaimed collections, beautiful poetry
not the usual tat that is continually rejected. Still,
it's all in the way you look at things, it's in the way
one's hand goes out, reaching for something beautiful,
a dry martini, nights on the Cote d'Azur, a moment
of success. Oh, that word *vermouth* still intoxicating
even in this 'residence', called 'home'.

CHRISTIAN WARD

The man who collects door knobs

hushes them to sleep like new-borns
before stroking their pampered
surfaces. A solid brass example
engraved with a sunbathing daisy.
A pair of bronze siblings decorated
with a serpentine weave. Solid
mahogany specimens longing
for the god rays filtering through
the rainforest's canopy. Others
are handled more carefully:
those made of crystal, embedded
with precious stones like a trophy
from *Indiana Jones*, or gold.
He admires a Victorian door knob
sculpted with a hypnotist's swirl
from afar. The nickel beehive
is kept under lock and key. Says
it buzzes at all hours, drives him
to do unspeakable things. His mother
speaks through the tentacle of a door
handle; her saline words like rotten honey.
Enough to make the door knobs wail,
ask where the rest of their bodies are.

CHRISTINE VIAL

Mugged

Shards of my favourite coffee mug
spill out onto the evening patio –
a stumble in the dark and something
else beautiful has been broken

at a time when all my morning mirror
has to offer me is a crazy-paving face.

Nor love, nor time, nor utilitarian glue,
nor Kintsugi gold, nor seven years bad luck,
nor all the kings' men, can put this
Humpty Dumpty back together again.

Instead, the open-mouthed bin yawns wide.
It's ready and waiting for the both of us.

JULIETTE HART

Downsizing

Each day I will discard something else
(a dining table, a box of diaries, a decanter)
until I'm left with just enough to fill an apartment.

I will get used to a new fall
                              of light

how the slant of blinds
            fabricates ladders
                        lacerates corners
                                    crimps patterns of leaves.

What will I miss?

Naked feet on carpeted stairs,
hanging washing on the line, following
the sun and the seasons around the garden. You.

EVE JACKSON

Robbery

He spread the last of the spent coffee grounds,
a handful of grit, sharp wood chips, now
copper wire wraps the broom's slender trunk.
Balletic stretch of gastropod wavers mid-air,
muscular lengthening reach, reached.

Daylight robbery; yellow catkins, baby
green-eyed leaves stripped. Tentacles wobble,
snail quivers at his pinch of finger and thumb. Plucked.

Years since he thought of walking on egg shells,
stealing past unnoticed. How, as a boy, leaning in
for a hug, the wizened body shivered at his touch.

Never quite able to grasp who this man was;
overhearing tales of slime-oozed drunkenness,
the late night deceits. And why this raking up the past
when there is bird song above the early summer jobs
and a yellow beak waits to complete the task.

TERRY JONES

The Compost

You were the sole begetter of our compost,
and I its faithful retainer,
its priest, gathering indulgences
to tip into the holy bin:
harvestings of lawn, hebdomadal
caddies of food waste – nothing to surprise you,
your dank teabags, voluminous leaves
and sturdy stalks of cauliflower –
rotting proof of proper eating –
plus cores and peelings various, and not even
pips and stones are beneath consideration.

In the lower bin strata which cover
a brace of years, I imagine
the peaty substance I am seeking,
black and odourless and friable,
ready mulch for the spreading.

Don't fret about the bonus ingredients
or snigger: our historical bank statements,
your correspondence with the utilities,
shredded into paper straw, admitted
because you were not there to say no.

I think we both caught, on Gardeners'
Question Time, the listener who spread
a silk blouse on her compost
and kept watch on its dissolution.

Perhaps I drifted out of earshot,
but I cannot recall her reasoning
or whether she felt she had succeeded
or failed. I know what you would think.

SUSAN JORDAN

A Life

Born, I learned to be lonely. My heart folded over on itself.

My name was loved but belonged to too many people.

My father blew a paper squeaker at me in my cot.
He sang *Where's that tiger?*

My mother's smile said everything was lovely,
even when it wasn't.

I loved lemon jelly and smeared it over me.
The wet crunch of mushrooms on toast.

Our house when we moved there: moss on the roof,
spiders in the garden.

Language unrolling from people's mouths,
the taste of words in mine.

My Grandmop was real. Why did she die so soon?
Her face was love.

The Coronation. Little grey people on Auntie Bessie's TV,
the gold coach in my scrapbook.

The atom bomb, creeping fear. Nuclear bunkers,
Strontium 90.

A man in space, and before him a dog. The Russians got there first.

Uncle Ruby found dead in his car. Coronary thrombosis.

Joey, our budgie, dead in his cage. He ate fertiliser
from the geraniums.

The Beatles at Finsbury Park Empire. In row U we couldn't see them.
I screamed anyway.

At school I grew up and didn't want to.
I wore stockings instead of socks and read *Middlemarch*.

My school boater was run over by a lorry. The top came off
like Popeye's can of spinach.

I left school and didn't know how to be a grown-up.
I still don't, but these days I don't try so hard.

Miss Austen does not like being sculpted

Such a great annoyance, having to stand still
and be gazed at by the likes of this man
who fancies himself a sculptor.

No longer pretty – if I ever was –
not wearing the dress I chose but one
he insisted on my wearing;

forbidden to write or sew, speak, smile or laugh
for this interminable time while his eyes –
his shameless, prying eyes –

examine each part of me, avoiding none.
He took away my shawl, tried to pull
my dress closer round my body.

If I were a dog I would have bitten him.
Patience, my dear Father would have said.
Think how pleasing the result

will be to us, your family. I know my sister
will dislike heartily the crude clay, the features
a travesty of mine, the body

all too obviously implied under its dress.
This is the last time I shall endure it.
Tomorrow I shall skewer him in my novel.

Recipe for a tor

Take heaps of stone
piled high like building blocks
put together by giant children.

Take granite stubble scattered
over grass, rough and uneven
as though the giants had got bored.

Mix in grass, tormentil, bell heather,
sheep droppings, wind fit to blow you over
as you cling to stone walls.

Turn to see hills tiled over with fields,
decorated with woods, houses bedded
into valleys, flat water glinting blue.

Smell air that has hardly been breathed
see clouds skating above you, ready
to lift you out of boggy ground.

Look at your feet, see how small you are.
Hear ravens grumble behind rocks,
watch sheep pondering the next mouthful.

Hear the silence of human voices stilled.
Let granite become your bones. Stretch your arms
as wide as the whole sky.

PENNY BLACKBURN

Through Harvested Fields

after Rob van Hoek

You are a line that might be sand
or might be road. You weave angel outlines

of ghost-backed birds.
The desire lines you created across me

are now barred by wire-and-wood fences,
hedgerow geometry. The furrows of my heart

are tractor torn. Across the landscape
apple-dot bales have parcelled summer's heat

into manageable neatness. I wait
between the harrowed earth,

the slate-slab sky. I am a scratch of pasture,
lost between tamed fields.

Clays

Soon it will be spring and something will draw us
into the woods, foraging for pigeon clays.
We'll scrabble among the scattered pieces,
raven-black or hi-viz orange concealed
under spreading aconites and swaying bluebells.
We'll compare our booty like pirates over treasure.
It's lucky to find one whole.

We'll make a day camp
under the small chalk cliff, build sticks
into a fire that we'll never light, under an old tin can
that's found half-buried. Lay out the pieces of clays,
first by size then into a pattern. We'll devise
an incantation, call up irresistible power.
Draw it from the land by the shape of the shells.

We'll sing, if the birds and the trees are listening.
We'll shout *Pull!* to each other over and over.

Stumbling Across the Pet Cemetery

In the woods
we find the little stones.
Like dry mushrooms, unseasonal,
popping through the grass.

Old markers,
whistling for ghost dogs.
Fingal, Callie, Cedric, Spot –
all come to heel a long time past.

I'm full of childish sorrow.
Wish I could have a pet,
so I could dig a loamy plot,
conduct a mournful service.

I turn to ask
but mum is busy, gripping Nanny,
holding her up. Nanny's nails
half-mooning mum's arms.

Her voice in anger, thick with tears:
"They buried these? These household pets?
And they wouldn't even give my boy
the lickings of a dog."

Later I will learn
of the sorrow before my mum was born.
How in a sterile hospital room
more than fifty years ago,

something broken was so swiftly taken away.
and Nanny's world closed over like a grave.

GLEN WILSON

Know a river by its sound

how each meander has its shout or *scairt*,
guldèr or *gowl*, it will find its own way,

singing erosion and rush in constant art,
vowels crash into consonants each day.

If you listen close enough, and I had to,
you can tell the difference in bodies of water,

how streams have accents for each season,
how they each speak with unique augur.

Trees worship its movement, from Oak root
to Ash sapling, bending and bowing

to creak with the wind in soft fiddle music,
each note reaches for the note that follows.

Dialect drives the thirsty current, brushing
aside the names we choose to call them

for something a little further up the course,
An Iascaigh, Eask, Eske, or made wet again

to be chanted on a seamless descant
of our descendant's lips. Wait. Listen. Heed.

Scairt – Irish - Shout
Guldèr – Ulster Scots – Yell
Gowl - Ulster Scots - Cry

TIM KEILY

Botany Lessons

I moved too often to learn the names
of flowers – never got beyond
the seasonal cycle of '*reds, blues and yellows*'
and the occasional charismatic cherry,

even while I made my way
from quad to quad, garden to garden,
ungrown in any courtesy
to my surroundings, until I stopped

somewhere under a corner of sky
whose bluebells and tulips and dandelions
would, year on year, become as close
to mine as could be managed. Let

the bog-water in the park and what
might be a lotus growing from it
give their instruction. You love a place
by learning to pay attention.

GARY DAY

About Daffodils

Daffodils used to be
So well behaved,
Knowing their place
Beside the lake, beneath the trees;
Yellow heads bent in deference
To the stars' greater fires;
A fluttering host greeting
The lonely poet floating
Over hills and dales,
Delighting him even
As he lay pensive on his couch,
Savouring the truths
That come from solitude.

The daffodils in my garden
Are a right bunch, spilling
Out like drunks from a bar,
Blowing their trumpets and
Shoving the snowdrops aside;
Some sway unsteadily while
Others fall flat on their faces.
These guys don't dance, much
Less flutter, nor do they take
Kindly to being stared at by poets.
I hide behind the couch but
Hear them shuffling closer;
Their huge manes flaring.

DAVID WYNNE-JONES

June Pollarding

You should pollard your tree every year when the tree is dormant, in late winter or very early spring.

There was something indecent about the way
the work crew stripped the tree
yelling and swarming over widespread arms,
slung from a rigging of ropes, helmeted
and visored, wielding chainsaws; violation
in the buzzing sawteeth, the rattling snarl
of mechanism masticating nests
and branchlets, spitting out a year's regrowth
into a trailer-load of woodchips, mulch,
as leaf litter blew along the street.

In the quiet aftermath, missed twigs
shivered a few last leaves, naked boughs
shook fingerless fists at the angry sky,
for weeks before drawing on green mittens
of new leafage, wrapping rags of raiment,
around scarred limbs while ferns colonised
the cracked brickwork of a nearby chimney-stack;
the same insurgency of vegetation
that splits concrete slabs, roots into tarmac
in the centre of little-used lanes.

Years ago, field margins where I walk
were planted with broad-leaved woodland,
native species, under the Set-aside Scheme.
Today I found a stand of cherry trees
laden with clusters of the sweet black fruit
and thought how hard it had been to protect,
on my smallholding, thirty years ago,
any such harvest from the depredations
of songbirds, listening in the silence now
to the wind's whisper; "Too little...too late."

DIANA CANT

Ash dieback

i
The ash trees are gone; those three great trees
that for years have framed my life, have been
my waking and my sleeping, the first and last shapes
on the threshold of my day. The house
lies vulnerable to passing eyes,
to neighbours curious about another's life;
my small scratchings on the surface of the soil
revealed, a garden hard-won from flint and chalk,
pleasure taken in a rose-bed, harebell and forget-me-not.

ii
You planted rare daffodils beneath those trees,
beguiling yellow-lime, snowdrops in the green,
a climbing rose, blood-red. How you live on,
as I work to reclaim them from the turmoil of the felling,
train the rose up another, healthy tree.
I watch a wren, beak-busy in the winter undergrowth,
while the dog sleeps nose to paw,
comma-curled before the fire.
Wind stirs in the chimney breast.

iii
The tree surgeon stops, kills the chain-saw,
says he wishes you could see the garden
now the trees are down; he recalls
a conversation ten years ago
when you had thought the ashes should be felled;
I had resisted, feeling it too soon.
As we speak, we side against regret, but agree
to wish things had happened differently.
I love that he remembered you.

JOHN PRIESTLEY

Silent Woodland

Silence of the emptiness when the hollow drumming of a woodpecker stops
   in the sheen on a beetle's carapace as it turns over a leaf

Silence in the interstices in the see-saw song of a chiff-chaff
   of the petal that floats down from a pollinated violet

Silence in the exhalation of an oak tree stirred by the breeze
   of the slow unfurling of a brown fern fiddlehead

Silence of the pause in the continuum of a cuckoo's call
   as a butterfly shadow descends on pink campion

Silence of the screeching indigo of bluebells in sunlight
   as a dandelion parasol drifts through stillness

Silence in the cascading notes of a song thrush song
   as a roe deer tiptoes through a sunlit glade

Silence of the leaf that drops from a birch branch
   of the soundless ascent of a tree-creeper

Silence in the afterwards of a fallen branch
  of thought
  of breathing
  in this wood
  alone

IRIS ANNE LEWIS

The Burry Man

Alone on the bridleway.
The path is blocked with brambles,
opulent with berries
bruising to black,
pressing their bittersweet fruit
into my mouth.
My lips, wanton and crimson,
run with juice.

Thorns scratch arms and face.
I push through. The path beyond
is lined with trees.
Go on, they whisper, *go on.*

The fields are packed with barley,
each ear pearled with grain.
On the borders a profusion of burdock,
their towering stems spiked with prickly heads.

They stick to my jeans and t-shirt;
they robe me in burrs.
I did not expect such generosity.

The barley ripples
gold, green, then grey,
becomes water, a lake, a loch,
the hedgerow a bank of thistles and pebbles.

A man, clothed in burrs, stalks towards me.
Our bodies cling fast together
and all I know
is the taste of his whiskey-breath.

WENDY KLEIN

The truth about cannibal ladybirds

Like a domestic version of the plague of locusts,
they come in through cracks and crevasses
we didn't know existed.

Orange and black and sudden, their dots too tiny
to count, to determine whether they are
foreign and should be squashed or deported,

or domestic, to be welcomed and admired.
They play dead so deftly, we can't decide
whether to attempt rescue,

or sweep them away, hoover them up,
but when I trap one between my fingers
it oozes yellow in protest,

and placed on the back of my hand
it bites, leaves a wound, small
as a pinprick, sharp as retaliation.

JENNA PLEWES

Sand

I see you, surf swirling round your ankles
                 dwarfed by an eternity of beach

your small body powdered with sand
                     mica glinting your bare feet
                     sand and salt rasping your wet skin

           later

I find more sand on the kitchen floor, sweep up
                   the slow grinding of millennia into grit

and smaller, infinitely small
                 the indelible stain of microplastic

that taints the loveliness of gorse, and oystercatchers,
                 hermit crabs and cowry shells

the sea smooths away your footprints, wind ruffles the dunes
               gulls scream,
                     unclean,
                           unclean
                               unclean
                                   unclean

TONY WATTS

From the Mainland

Mile upon mile of library shelves play host
to a whispering dust – it is the ghost
of every tale no longer told
one to another in the firelit circle.

TV cameras shepherd to my room
enough wildlife to scupper Noah's Ark
a hundred times over, yet there is no beast
I'd hunt or harbour or
take as totem on the spirit's journey.

Courtesy of fibre-optics I can name
all the gods of humankind, yet none
I'd worship or entreat; I can look in
on feasts and festivals around the world
and never join the dance.

We're wallflowers all –
sated tourists picnicking among
our own ruins.

The cosmos is in flight
from its centre. Men follow,
fleeing theirs. Nothing can appease them
short of the unapproachable god
to which the unnamed stars
come no closer than the toddler who one day
makes it to the garden gate.

I'd like to be an island poet,
somewhere off the coast of Scotland.
I would cast my song like a net, trawl in
those images – the lark on the hill,
the boat in the bay. My verses (known
to fisherman and laird alike) would show
how the eternal is not found
in the far distances of space and time,
but simply in knowing how to be at home
within the magic circle of the sea.

IAIN McCLURE

Landing in Belfast

The descent is through clouds
westward to the dark hills
along a coast of yesterdays

Headlands on the port side
outcrops of fractal rock
citadels of seabirds

An island where I lay down
in long summer grasses
when the sun stood still

Redbrick school façades
suburban streets, playing fields
care homes, our old house

an Airbnb now
white walls turning green
roses neglected

Family ashes gather
in civic, numbered rows
on a high slope to the south

There will be a final time
for me to land in drizzle
in a place once my home

There will be an ending
to this country of first kisses
the land of last goodbyes

The Old Ways

Young Dolan never listened:
Straight after his da's requiem
He grubbed out the fairy tree
That stood on the hillside
Of ancient stone and buckled whin
All the townland knew.

As soon as that hawthorn burnt,
All the milk from Dolan's herd
Pinked with blood in the pail.
His lambs were all stillborn -
One had an eyeless head.
Every night his front door shook,
Even when the wind was still.
Next, the back door too -
Fever in its bolts.

Speaking many tongues,
Young Dolan was led away
One black Sunday morning
By Patterson, the doctor -
A kind man, though a protestant.

We stared at our pints
In Mooney's bar on Monday
Reflecting on the old ways,
How they are not mocked,
Put coins in collection tins
For families of the volunteers
In Long Kesh and Maghaberry -
And did not ask what Murphy's boys
Had hidden in the byre.

GARETH ROBERTS

Armadale

An autumn sea
crumples to the beach
and sighs across the little curve of Armadale,

laps at the lips of a footprint
left for a whirlpool
to scuttle a storm-battled crab-Columbus
in its ragged frigate of weed.

Abused by the breeze
this is the place where seagulls practice their bigotries,
mock the sheep
that drift insensible as storm clouds
through the crab's frail fleet, flapping

with the unlashed sail of skirts
that play around her like a child.
She tears a smile through her face
as her hand grasps the hands of the wind:
coughs a gull-like 'Amen!'
Rain cloud eyes blinking at nothing
that she can see with them.

While Columbus battles on through his storm,
through the whirlpools of footprints
kept, for a moment,
between the tides.

MICHAEL HENRY

Luftpost

The start of a Cold War friendship –
launching paper aeroplanes
in a compartment on the S-Bahn.
One landed in the lap of an East German –

so Volkmar became the fifth musketeer
with Ian, Coralie, Marimar and me.

Much later I visited Ian in Victoria.
His wife made home-made pasta,
he plucked his pawnshop banjo
and showed me letters from the GDR.

They went with his East German memorabilia
under the counter – like pornography.

And I wondered how Volkmar's huge hands
that worked with delicate optical equipment
could write with undulations in strait-laced script.
All the angst in the GDR was in his face.

Petrified of eavesdroppers he'd made us eat up
every drop of Communist soup with gristle and carrots.

I visited him after reunification.
He ate the leftovers off the plates.

DENISE BENNETT

Commemoration 2018

6,000 servicemen from Portsmouth died in WW1 1914 – 1918

Rows of terraced houses in Portsmouth
stand like soldiers on parade, a battalion.
On lampposts in over eight hundred streets
there are temporary plaques to mark the deaths.
Sidney Goad who fell, aged seventeen,
lived at eighteen Henderson Road;
Private 4805 signed up underage
lied his way to Mesopotamia,
the heat, disease, the lack of rations.
Did he miss home, swish of sea on the beach,
ducking under the washing in the yard,
dog barking, warming himself by the hearth,
his mother pouring tea from the brown pot?
Did he die from wounds, sickness, was he shot?

Singing for her

She was a country child, one of six.
She was the hands that milked the cows.
She was a chorister at eight, sang like a linnet.
She was the housemaid at the big house.
She was the girl who fell in love with a sailor,
left her Devon hamlet for a naval city.
She was a war widow left with a nine-week old son;
her husband blown to bits by a German sub.
She was a pauper, destitute, struggled for money
for bread to feed her child, herself.
She was a woman who scrubbed and cleaned
for rich women.
She was a pretty redhead who thought she'd
found love again, someone to trust.
She was the unmarried mother, a fallen woman,
left pregnant, deserted.
She was the one they shunned in her shame,
almost forced to give up her baby.
the one the matron bullied with adoption forms.
She was the strong woman who fled, escaped
to her family in the country.
She was the one whose brother and sister
opened their arms and held us close.
She was the one who fielded the stones thrown,
who fought long years with schizophrenia.
She was the one who at the end, wanted
the hymn, *Abide With Me.*
I was the one, her daughter, who lifted
up my voice and sang for her.

TINA COLE

To a House We Once Lived In

I suppose I should thank you for opening
your doors allowing us to break crusts
on the eyelids of old histories, beneath
the twenty or so colours sandpapered away.

For rusted windows flung puppet wide,
mapped in rain and frames swollen tight shut,
forced, tugged, hammered. The ladybirds
which bled among the hinges soon displaced.

For streets of houses handcuffed together,
coalman, *rag and bone*. Silver fish tickled
from the cast iron bath, the many luxury
soakings in three kettles of hot water.

The substance of years, so many nights between
cold walls, stuck between floorboards like hairpins,
chills gathering softly at the top of the stairs,
in corners where the carpet did not reach.

Blackbirds in the apple tree, a scritter of mice
in the attic. Wet days when the sky was a scum
skimming the canal, burst pipes, drains overflowing.
The two-bar electric fire the only welcome home.

HEATHER MOULSON

The Emotional Pantry

An emotional pantry is the best place
for cooling things down.
Leftovers once hot and intense sit there,
in a bewildered after-glow, smoking.
Lovesick jellies upon the next shelf
wobble forlornly.
Tins of anchovies and sardines self-contained
and unmoved sit primly above
frustrated packets of Angel Delight who long
to display their gaudy sugary colours.
Jars of artichokes and pickled onions carry
their own private and tumultuous pungency.
Table salt and industrial pepper sit complacently
side by side.
Old warriors. Seeing it all before.
Like the hardened granulated sugar opposite
or the world-weary wholemeal flour,
battling constantly with uninvited weevils.
They've witnessed these needy ingredients come and go.
Of course, things get soured by the occasional chicken carcass
left there a day too long under white mesh.
Stunning the edible inhabitants at how little it all takes.

SARAH DAS GUPTA

Returning to the House that Jack Built
(reflections 1942–2024)

Iron gates guard and forbid trespassing from the past,
No place to start again or peer deep into the earth itself;
only now, suddenly, sunlight reaches down, piercing the concrete –
releasing children's voices from a dark shrubbery,
the scent of grass and whine of a lawnmower.

Go through the door into the hall's darkening gloom.
The smell of dogs, wet fur from a sudden shower, beeswax,
 old carpets rising through layers of the excavated past.
The tip of the trowel only discovers, uncovers, half a portrait:
 grey, distorted, another country, too far, no passport.
 Keep to the edge of the abyss, roped safely to the now.

Look out through the kitchen window
beneath the now neatly gravelled parking lots.
At the very edge of memory, an oak tree is bare and leafless.
Then a snowy whiteness, stabbed with marks of blood and corpses.
Headless chicken, burst intestines, life seeping away into snow.
A fox disappears into darkness, dragging a mangled carcass.
Above Messerschmitts and Spitfires slit open winter skies.

Upstairs, enter a first world: images are childish,
stickmen walk up straight paths to red front doors.
Coils of grey smoke drift upwards, from chimneys,
defying the sun smiling from the topmost corner!
Now on the precipice of memory:
long, summer evenings, laughter
drifting in from neighbouring gardens,
the last cutting of hay – lost hours, searching for sleep!

The attic: forgotten headlines yellowing into papery dust:
a robin's nest, tufts of moss, interwoven,
aborted lives of a forgotten Spring.
Skylight. tightly locked. No flying free.

ALISON CAMPBELL

Look at my mother's bones that I carry

the tibia wrapped in a witch hazel bandage
I carry her radius and ulna strained and weak

from holding me when I was small.
She cleaned the house as I hung on to her

shrinking from the roar of the Hoover
the warm smell of the bag wheezing its carpet dust

I'm carrying her orbital bone now
fractured when the folding bed sprang open

I lift her skull –
rearrange the strands of hair, cover the bareness

I miss watching her do handstands

I hold her hands now in my mind
my fingers over hers, stroke

the loose creases of skin covering her knuckles
that softness of flesh

GERALD KILLINGWORTH

Her Last Snow

Soft and endless,
the snow gathers in crazy drifts,
maverick sculptures defying every guess.

Tell me about the garden she says.
Has the fox called yet, padding its signature?
What transformations?

She rests below the level of the window,
watching modest pyramids grow on the sill
and the snow falling, falling,
distracting her from other urgent things.

It's my last snow she says.
I'm so glad they managed it.

She has drawn her own white sheet
over all those years,
given the last determined smile,
a touch of the fingers –
Darling, may I leave now?

Her last Spring and Summer went unnoticed,
so too the birthdays,
but the snow brings a peace and silence
we, in our grief,
shall struggle to achieve.

DAVID HALE

Ghormeh Sabzi

For Nissa

You're lying in bed
listening to the rain you so love,
sure you can smell onions frying out there in the dark,
leading you back across land and sea

to your mother's kitchen on the edge of Meshed,
to crushed parsley and coriander, sauteed garlic
and fenugreek, dried limes, diced lamb

and the spill of red beans softened but not yet falling apart
in the long, gentle simmer of stew drifting
through the house, your mother standing by the door

transfigured by the sheer spring light, as she looks out
past the pomegranate and almond trees towards
the mountains beyond; O your mother

and her wonderful Ghormeh Sabzi, you can't help
thinking about her, trying not to feel tearful as you lie
listening to the endless blessing of this northern rain.

TIM KEILY

There Is No God, and He Is Always With You

(*after Seamus Heaney*)

'*Bright puddle, where the soul-free*
cloud-life roams' – this holds
even for those long since made
agreeable to the open space

where a soul would be; to the dawn sky
emptying and filling,
its plough-shaped flock of birds
now coasting, now diving askew, about

who-knows-what errands
not concerning you?

ABOUT THE POETS

Rosie Barrett has lived in South Devon since 1985 and doesn't regret a moment. Now on an estuary she loves the changing scene and the mud. Shortlisted to the Bridport, widely anthologised, One fifth of Called to the Edge she loves Open Mics and Zooms all over the world.

Denise Bennett has an MA in creative writing and teaches poetry workshops in community settings. She is widely published and has four poetry collections: *Planting the Snow Queen* and *Parachute Silk*, by Oversteps Books, *Water Chits* by Indigo Dreams and *Things I have kept*, published by Cinnamon Press in August 2024.

Penny Blackburn's poetry has featured in many journals and anthologies, including *Spelt, Riggwelter* and *Phare* and she was the winner of Poetry Tyne 2023. She has released her debut collection with Yaffle Press, *Gaps Made of Static.* She is on X and Facebook as @Penbee8.

Alison Campbell, from Aberdeen, lives in London. She has poems in publications, including *Pennine Platform, The Curlew, The Poetry Village, London Grip, Artemis* and *Indigo Dreams,* she was shortlisted for the Geoff Stevens Memorial Poetry Prize, and won the South Downs Poetry Competition both in 2023.

Diana Cant, joint editor of The Alchemy Spoon, won the Plaza Poetry Prize and was nominated for a Forward Prize in 2023. Her third pamphlet, *I make you bird,* is forthcoming with Broken Sleep, following *Student Bodies, 1968* (Clayhanger Press) and *At Risk – the lives some children live (*Vole Books).

Tina Cole has three published pamphlets, *I Almost Knew You*, (2018) and *Forged*/ Yaffle Press, (2021) and *What it Was* /Mark Time Books (2023). She has won and been placed in national poetry competitions and is widely published in magazines and collections. She completed an M.A. in creative writing at Manchester Metropolitan University in 2023.

Gary Day is a retired English lecturer. The author of several books on literary history, including The Story of Drama, he was also a columnist for The Times Higher. His poetry has appeared in Beyond Words and Acumen. His poem on Anne Brontë was highly commended in this year's Artemesia Poetry Competition.

Andrew George was born and lives in London where he works as a barrister. His debut collection, *Milk Round,* was published by Live Canon in 2015. His poems have appeared in *Magma* and *The Rialto.* He is Chair of Trustees of the charity, *Modern Poetry in Translation.*

Sharron Green has published Introducing Rhymes_n_Roses; Viral Odes & Willing Words. She has an MA in Creative Writing from the University of Surrey & has been Head Writer for their New Writer's Festival. She hosts monthly open mics & is a member of The Booming Lovelies, a trio of performing poets. To find out more go to https://linktr.ee/rhymes_n_roses

Sarah Das Gupta is from Cambridge. She has also lived and worked in India and Tanzania and her work has been published in over twenty countries from New Zealand to Kazakhstan and been placed in poetry competitions, including the Bermuda Triangle Prize.This year she is nominated for Best of the Net and a Dwarf Star Award.

David Hale was born in Scotland but now lives in Gloucestershire. He teaches refugees and asylum seekers English. He has published pamphlets with Happenstance and Templar and a collection with Eyewear.

Janet Hatherley's pamphlet, *What Rita Tells Me,* and collection, *On the road to Cadianda*, were both published by Dempsey & Windle/Vole in 2022 and in April this year. She has poems in several magazines, including *Under the Radar* and *Culture Matters*, winning 2nd prize in Enfield Poetry competition, 2023. @JanHatherley

Juliette Hart has been placed in the Jersey Festival of Words and Guernsey Poetry Competitions, and longlisted in the National Poetry Competition. She's read her poems in castles, bunkers, museums, dolmens, art galleries, operas, art houses in the Channel Islands, and in London at Torriano Meeting House and theTroubadour.

Michael Henry has published four collections with Enitharmon Press and one with Five Seasons Press. At the moment he is trying to find a publisher for his latest collection, *Brightness at Midnight*. He has been widely published in magazines.

Eve Jackson's poems have appeared widely in journals and anthologies. A past winner of the Frogmore Poetry Prize, winner of the Brian Dempsey single poem and Vole summer poetry competitions. A runner-up in Manchester Cathedral competition and author of three non-fiction books.

Terry Jones is a poet, editor, workshop leader based in Windsor. His work has recently appeared in *Poetry News* and on www.poeticvoices.live and East Anglian Bylines. Member of Reading Stanza and Ver Poets where he is the Competitions Secretary.

Susan Jordan has an MA in Creative Writing from Bath Spa University and has been writing poetry seriously since 2014 She has published two full-length collections and two pamphlets and her work has appeared in various magazines and anthologies. Her novel *The Box* was published in August 2024.

Tim Keily (photo: Tyrone Lewis) is a criminal barrister and writer based in London. He is the author of three poetry pamphlets including, most recently, *No Other Life,* a winner of the Brian Dempsey Memorial Competition 2023. Buy his books on timkielybooks.bigcartel.com.

Gerald Killingworth writes novels (mostly fantasy) for adults and children. *The Dead World of Lanthorne Ghules* (Pushkin, 2019) was a Guardian pick of the month. He has a Phd in Elizabethan literature and has had plays produced on the London fringe. Dempsey & Windle published Gerald's collection *Emptying Houses* in July 2022.

Wendy Klein once won first prize in the Ware Poetry Competition, the Cinnamon Press Single Poem, the Cannon Poets Sonnet or not, plus others. With 3 collections, a Selected and a pamphlet based on her great grandfather's letters as a Confederate Officer during the US Civil War, she's musing on a 4th collection.

Gill Learner, born in 1939 near Birmingham, now lives in Reading. Her poetry has won several awards including the Poetry Society's Hamish Canham Prize (2008), the Buxton (2011, 2012) and the Welsh (2024). Her collections are *The Agister's Experiment*, *Chill Factor* and *Change*, from Two Rivers Press, Reading, all positively reviewed.

Iris Anne Lewis is featured in Black Bough Poetry. Winner of the Gloucestershire Poetry Society and Graffiti competitions. Highly commended in the Wales Poetry Award 2022 and the Stanza competition 2023. She has read at the Cheltenham Literary Festival and has been a guest poet at the Cheltenham Poetry Festival.

Iain McClure grew up in the North of Ireland during the Troubles. He now lives and works in the South East of England teaching English and Politics. He started writing poetry again during the Covid-19 lockdown of 2020 after a hiatus of several decades.

Paul McDonald taught at the University of Wolverhampton for twenty five years, before taking early retirement in 2019. He is the author of 20 books to date, which include fiction, poetry and scholarship. His most recent poetry collection is *60 Poems* (Greenwich Exchange Press, 2023)

Heather Moulson has performed extensively in London and Surrey. She was a winner of the Brian Dempsey Memorial Award 2019, and had a pamphlet *Bunty, I Miss You* published by Dempsey & Windle that year. She is also part of The Booming Lovelies with two other poets, who performed at the Guildford Fringe 2023.

Sue Norton has had poems published in various magazines and anthologies. She has won prizes in the Rialto Nature competition, the Poetry Society Members' competition, and the York and Enfield competitions, and has been commended in many more. Sue is a member of the York stanza.

Jenna Plewes has published 6 poetry collections and three pamphlets. Her poems appear in journals and several anthologies. *A Lick of Loose Threads* came out in 2023, and *Holding the Light* in 2024. Both are sold in aid of Doctors without Borders. Contact her at jenna.selvas@googlemail.com

John Priestley lives in SW Scotland and has been writing since he first put chalk to slate. After 10 years in Edinburgh, a year travelling in Asia and a stint in Singapore he has settled to life in beautiful Galloway. He has been "managing" the local Poetry Group since 2007.

Gareth Roberts lives in Aberystwyth and has had poems published in various journals and anthologies, including: *Aesthetica, Poetry Space, Orbis, Allegro, Envoi, Acumen, South* and *Welsh Poetry Competition Anthology*. He has published a collection, entitled *What's Not Wasted* (Tawny Owl Press, 2016); and presents live performances in concert with experimental musicians.

Derek Sellen lives in Canterbury and has written poetry over many years. He writes: I remembered haggling in markets in India and Turkey while writing 'The Merchant in Autumn'. I once bought some beautiful sari material for a friend and in the poem imagined a woman encountering a persuasive merchant.

Tricia Torrington is a poet, printmaker and maker of artists books. She has one collection published by Flarestack and is currently working on a second collection. She often puts poetry into art books.

Christine Vial – teacher, writer, social activist - grew up in London's Eastend and now lives in Enfield, North London, with her American artist husband. Pamphlet: *Dancing in Blue Flip-flops* (RQ press 2018). Recent publications: Poetry Society newsletter; *Poems for the Year 2020* (Shoestring Press); Barnet and Enfield Poets anthologies; website/podcast celebrating Enfield industry.

Christian Ward is a London-based poet with two collections, *Intermission* and *Zoo,* available on Amazon and elsewhere: His work has appeared in numerous literary journals and was longlisted for the 2023 National Poetry Competition and recognised this year in the Maria Edgeworth, Pen to Print, London Independent Story and Shahidah Janjua Poetry Competitions.

Anthony Watts has been writing 'seriously' for more than fifty years. He has won over eighty prizes in poetry competitions and has had poems published in many magazines and anthologies. His latest collection is *Stiles* (Paekakariki Press). His main interests are poetry, music, walking, binge thinking and being a great-grandad.

Rod Whitworth, born in 1943, has done a number of jobs. He currently works as a medical rôle-player. He lives in Oldham and is still tyrannised by commas. His collection, *My Family and Other Birds*, was published in 2024.

Glen Wilson won the Seamus Heaney Award for New Writing 2017, the Jonathan Swift Creative Writing Award 2018 and Goldsmith Poetry Competition 2024. His poetry collection *An Experience on the Tongue* is out now. Twitter @glenhswilson

Dave Wynne-Jones left teaching for health reasons, gaining an MA in creative writing at MMU, then writing articles for outdoor magazines and organising expeditions for mountaineers. He's published two books of mountaineering non-fiction and two poetry pamphlets, whilst his poems have also been anthologised and appeared in magazines.

Dónall and Janice Dempsey have been publishing poetry collections
and competition anthologies since 2016,
mostly under their original imprint,
Dempsey & Windle.

Since January 2023, they have been publishing exclusively under
their new imprint,
VOLE Books.

All their books can be ordered, through their website
and from any good independent bookshop.

VOLE Books
dempseyandwindle@gmail.com
dempseyandwindle.com
@VOLEbooks
www.facebook.com/VOLEbooks/